T5-BQA-673

FAITH
NOT
FEAR

COURAGE TO
IMPACT CULTURE

DR. GERALD STOW

Faith Not Fear

Dr. Gerald Stow

Vision Leadership Foundation
Brentwood, TN

Faith Not Fear by Dr. Gerald Stow

©Copyright 2016 Vision Leadership Foundation. All Rights Reserved.

Any form of duplication—physical, digital, photographic or otherwise is expressly forbidden, unless authorized in writing by the author/publisher.

ISBN 978-0-9904033-7-1

Scripture quoted in this book comes from one of the four sources noted below. In many cases, the Scriptures were translated or paraphrased by Dr. Stow himself.

Scripture taken from Holman Christian Standard Bible. Copyright © 1999, 2000, 2002, 2003, 2009 by Holman Bible Publishers (HCSB). Used with permission by Holman Bible Publishers, Nashville, Tennessee. All rights reserved.

Scripture taken from the KING JAMES VERSION (KJV), public domain.

Scripture taken from the NEW AMERICAN STANDARD BIBLE® (NASB), Copyright © 1960, 1962, 1963, 1968, 1971, 1972, 1973, 1975, 1977, 1995 by The Lockman Foundation. Used by permission.

Scripture taken from THE HOLY BIBLE, NEW INTERNATIONAL VERSION®, NIV® Copyright © 1973, 1978, 1984, 2011 by Biblica, Inc.® Used by permission. All rights reserved worldwide.

Table of Contents

Acknowledgements

This book would never been possible without the valuable assistance of Brian Ball, George Bright, Leon Drennan, and Jim and Val Harvey.

This team provided technical support as well as theological correctness. Thanksgiving is given to the Vision Leadership Foundation, for without it this book would never have been possible.

Dedication

It is with great delight that I dedicate this writing to my long time friends Jim and Val Harvey.

These friends have not only been an inspiration but have provided great role models for writing and living out lives in *Faith Not Fear*.

Introduction

America has always been recognized as a country with courage. The spirit of courage was in the founding fathers of this nation. That courage was drawn from the Word of God. Men and women faced adversity on every hand as a nation was born. But our nation today has seen a tremendous shift away from these values.

A recent event in our world demonstrates what happens when we do not take a courageous stand. After the fall of the leader of Iraq, our nation spent billions of dollars in arming and training their citizens in how to be courageous in battle. Then they came face to face with the enemy, and the video was there for the entire world to see. The Iraqi citizens threw down their arms and ran away from the battle. What a shame. They did not have the courage to face the culture and the conflict.

John was instructed by Christ "to write about what you have seen, what is, and what will take place hereafter." (Revelation 1:19). So Christ had John write a message to each of the seven churches of Asia. He revealed an attribute about Himself in order to encourage the church to meet the challenge of changing their culture. The Revelation of Jesus Christ is the only place in the Bible where Jesus directly shares the message (II Peter 1:27). The seven churches listed in Revelation 2 and 3 were literal churches. However, many feel each church also represents a period of time in church history (Barnes; Morgan; Stott; Strauss; Talbot; Weiss, Jeremiah). The historical evidence surrounding the various churches at the time of John's writing certainly identifies with the historical evidence of the church age. There are others who do not share this position. Since the Lord Jesus is telling John what to write, He and He alone could foresee the entire church age from its beginning to its closure. *"Known unto God are all his works from the beginning of the age."* (Acts 15:18 KJV).

These churches faced much adversity from the culture outside and from the membership inside. The message Christ spoke to the people in the seven churches helped them to face the issues of their day. These messages were good then, and they are relevant for our culture today.

The Writer

John was a prisoner on the island of Patmos. He was placed there by the Roman Empire for his influential ministry for Christ. In the Revelation of Jesus Christ we find a different approach than in other Scripture. In this final book of our Bible it is Christ who gives the Word, not the Spirit. Christ chooses seven churches—the perfect and complete number. He is pictured as standing in the midst of them. He is there for each church to see, unifying them into one whole, and directing them by individual messages, showing His intimate acquaintance with the details of each.

In the midst of the darkness of the world's night, Jesus says there are seven lampstands.[1] Lampstands are instruments to hold light to dispel darkness. These stands are not the source of the light, but they hold and support the light. They differ from a candle light, for that type of light is used up and has to be replaced. The light on these lampstands was fueled with oil. Oil is symbolic of the Spirit. The lampstand is identified by Christ as the church. Jesus said, *"I am the light of the world."* (John 9:5 KJV).

When a church is totally focused on Jesus, then the light of Christ shines through the members, dispelling the darkness. We have no light of our own to fight the darkness, so God's light must shine through us if we are to impact the dark culture around us.

John had been exiled to the Isle of Patmos for standing on the Word of God and the testimony he gave of Jesus. Jesus gives him a vision of the glorified Christ, and he is to write about what he saw. He sees the glorified Christ standing in the circle of the seven churches. He is described as walking amidst these churches and holding the pastors in His right hand.

Jesus is the unchanging Christ: *"Jesus Christ the same yesterday, today and forever."* (Hebrews 13:8). Today, He still walks amidst the churches and holds church leadership in His right hand—the place of power and security. In many instances today, churches with itching ears and wandering eyes are looking everywhere but not on Jesus. They are looking at the buildings, the size of the membership, and the latest technology, but they have not turned their light on the darkness around them. The Church is the bride of Christ, and it is during the engagement period that she is to make herself ready for the day when her groom, Jesus, will come to claim her.

This preparation time must be filled with the church reaching into the darkness and shining the light of love to the unbelievers. In the face of our enemy, we must not lay down our weapons of prayer, the Word, our spiritual gifts, and our witness to His saving power.

The problems faced by the seven churches of Asia are being repeated every day. May God help us to fight the good fight of faith that was once delivered to the saints.

The need of the hour is for every believer to rise up by sharing the good news that Christ is the only hope for a degenerate culture. It is a call for the church to stand up and defend the faith once delivered to the saints by declaring that the Bible is the inspired, living Word of God. The challenge is for the church to speak up and state that God is a holy God and that His followers need to practice holiness in their daily living if they are to impact their culture. Christ said to one of the seven churches that He was coming back as a thief in the night, so they should be ready. Are you ready should He come back today?

<u>The Plan</u>

The writer was impressed to choose the title "Faith not Fear" because of his personal belief that it is with our faith that we become more than conquerors. There was a house parent at the Tennessee Baptist Children's Home that was diagnosed with cancer and in a few months experienced her home going. Since 1986 they had been the parents for over 200 children. As she faced this terminal illness she adopted the theme "Faith not Fear." Recent events in our nation and in the world at large where innocent people are being slaughtered have created a climate and culture of fear. To stand against this, God has given us the weapon of faith. A simple definition of this word when used as an acrostic is: **Forsaking All I Trust Him.** At the conclusion of each chapter there is a study guide to enable the readers to utilize their faith in changing the culture in their world.

The writer has followed a format of giving an introduction to what Christ is saying to the church, followed by a history of the city where the church is located, since most churches will take on the culture of their surroundings. The outline continues with the "attribute" Jesus reveals of Himself as He addresses the issues faced in each church. Jesus commended most of the churches, but also expressed condemnation. Finally the Application is made as a "take away" from each church. The reader can look for Introduction, History, Attribute, Commendation, or Condemnation, and finally Application in each discussion of the seven churches. Some will not necessarily follow this exact order, but will be inclusive according to purpose and need.

Chapter 1

MAKING THE MAIN THING
THE MAIN THING

~

The Church at Ephesus
(Revelation 2:1-7)

Introduction

God gave the story of how it all began to Moses in the book of Genesis. The Revelation of Jesus Christ was given to John to tell us how it all will end. Revelation is a book of prophecy. It also is a book that tells us how we can impact our culture for mankind's good and Christ's glory.

Christ reveals Himself to John in His glorified state as walking among the churches and holding the church leadership by His right hand (Rev. 1:16, 20). He selects seven churches in Asia Minor and addresses each one individually. He gives words of commendation and, in some cases, condemnation. In doing so, He reveals a different attribute of Himself, which is the basis for meeting their need. A focus on these attributes will provide a source of encouragement and help for today's needs. He then concludes each statement by telling them, *"Anyone who has an ear should listen to what the Spirit says to the churches."* (Rev. 2:7).

Many feel that these were seven literal churches. A careful study shows that each church in a progressive order represented a particular period in church history. The following theologians hold this view: Barnes; Morgan; Stott; Strauss, Talbot and Jeremiah. John was given a prophetic view of the whole church age from Pentecost to the return of Christ, seeing the end of the church age from the beginning. Each one of the seven churches reflects the particular problem faced within their place in the history of the church age.

The problems addressed then are problems believers face today. A discovery of these problems and the solution offered by our Lord will enable the believers of today to have the courage to impact the present culture.

<u>History</u>

The first church addressed by the risen Savior was Ephesus whose name means "desirable" (Rev. 2:1-7). This church represents the apostolic age of church history.[2] It was an exciting time when the gospel message was being shared throughout the world. The church at Ephesus was a church that worked hard, was patient in suffering, and sound in doctrine—a desirable church, but she had left her first love. The attribute Jesus revealed was that He is *"The One who holds the seven stars in His right hand and who walks among the seven gold lamp stands."* (Rev. 2:1).

Ephesus was by far the greatest city of the province of Asia Minor. The city has been called "the light of Asia" and the "vanity fair" of the ancient world. What gave this place its greatness? At the time of John's writings, Ephesus, with its rivers, roads, and harbor's was the gateway to all of Asia. All travel and commerce by land and water converged on this city. Traffic in merchandise and men made it the wealthiest city in the world.[3]

It was also the center of worship of Diana of the Ephesians, one of the Seven Wonders of the World. This temple of Diana, the most impressive and spectacular seventh wonder, was located here. The structure was 425 feet wide with 130 columns, 60 feet high in rows of twos, each the gift of a king. Thirty-seven of these columns were embellished with colors of red, gold, scarlet, and blue.

In the center of the temple was the most beautiful and impressive altar in the world. Beyond the altar hung a gorgeous veil made of velvet. Beyond this veil was the shrine of the goddess Diana. Beyond this shrine was an inner shrine, which housed all the sacred things of the nation.

The temple also was a place of refuge for criminals. At this site, lawbreakers were free from arrest and prison and beyond the law. The temple served as a place for religious asylum.

Pilgrims came to Ephesus by the thousands. The temple keepers sold little images of the goddess Diana. The people carried the idols and put them in their houses and on chariots for good luck. The immorality of Diana worship was indescribable.

Scores of eunuchs, thousands of temple prostitutes, and thousands of singers and dancers worked themselves up into a pagan immoral frenzy. The morals of the temple were worse than animals.

Our Lord said, *"Except thou repent I will remove thy lampstand."* (Rev. 2:5). In 252 A.D. the Goths destroyed the temple and the city. The area never recovered. The great ruins of the temple were used as a quarry for the beautification of Constantinople. Centuries of floods, along with grass and weeds, have filled up the blue lagoon of the Cayster River. The inhabitants of the city have fled. The great amphitheater is a total ruin. A stagnant pond of water covered with green scum occupies the site where the temple once stood. Frogs croak in the night, "Great was Diana."

When John wrote this letter and when Paul preached in Ephesus for three years, no one ever dreamed that this great city would soon perish from the earth. Ephesus was the most unlikely place in the world for Christianity to be planted. Yet in this city, Christianity had some of its greatest triumphs. Not only was Ephesus a great city, but also a great church was established there. So for a church that had lost their focus and left their first love, what attribute does Christ offer to meet their needs?

First, we have to define what is meant by "first love." Jesus tells us that "first love" is to *"Love the Lord your God with all your heart, with all your soul, with your entire mind, and with all your strength."* (Mark 12:30). Paul expressed it when he wrote saying, *"For me to live is Christ."* (Phil. 1:21). To seek His glory and not our own selfish desires— this is the first love of the child of God.

Attribute

To confront the problem, Jesus reveals Himself as the one who holds the seven stars (pastors, church leaders) in His right hand and is walking among His churches.

Jesus was never the loner. He was always involving Himself with the rich and the poor, the Jew and the Gentile, the religious and the irreligious. Community was important to Him as He demonstrated by the calling of the disciples. Within that twelve, He also selected three—Peter, James and John—for a more intimate community.

When God created Adam, He observed that it was not good for man to be alone, so He created Eve to walk along the side of Adam as his helpmate. To this union were born three children: Cain, Abel and Seth. Later, other children were born to the first family, enlarging the community (Gen. 5:4). So the first family was established as the first earthly community. When Adam and Eve disobeyed God, He came "walking" and looking for them. He was revealing His Presence and Power as the God of Holiness who was full of love and compassion for the family community He had created. Christ continues to walk alongside dads and moms and their children. In His Word He has set forth some high standards for the family (Ephesians 5-6).

God's Word clearly defines His definition of family. *"This is why a man leaves his father and mother and bonds with his wife, and they become one flesh."* (Gen. 2:24). The family as God planned it is under attack. Families are the basic foundation in our nation. In recent days, the nation with its warped culture has redefined family by the recognition of "same sex marriage." Violence has erupted over the Planned Parenthood organization for performing abortions—the taking of innocent lives. God's Word clearly defines His definition of family: *"This is why a man leaves his father and mother and bonds with his wife, and they become one flesh."* (Gen. 2:24).

God is a longsuffering, patient, and compassionate God. But how long will God put up with the church of this age that has failed to change the culture that condones horrible acts of the murder of innocent infants, murder of innocent victims by drive-by shootings, greed on Wall Street, neglect of the poor, turning away of the stranger (immigrant), neglect of the Word of God in the houses of God, idol worship and the heresy of distorting the true Word of God, and failure to recognize Jesus Christ as the Savior of the world?

Could it be that the drastic change in weather problems, the wild fires in the western states destroying natural resources, the hard winters in the northeast, the drastic rise in violent crimes against humanity, and the acts of terrorism are all the foreshadowing of the tribulation that is prophecy to come in the future? The church will not be here when the Seven years of Tribulation comes.[4] When John hears the voice in John 4:1 that says *"Come up here,"* He is speaking, not only to John, but to every believer on the face of the earth at that time (I Thess. 4:13-18). This is not the second coming of Christ, for that will not happen until the seven years of Tribulation takes place on the earth. Meanwhile, in Heaven some wonderful things are taking place. Remember that Jesus is the groom, and the church is His bride (Eph. 5:25-33). We, as His bride, should certainly be excited about what we will one day experience.

During the weeks and months of planning for a wedding, the most exciting person is the bride. There is the preparation and choice of the right clothing to wear, the invitation of relatives and guests, and a thousand and one other details. The day of the wedding arrives, and the bride is ushered in on the arm of the Father. The eyes of the bride are on the groom who is anxiously awaiting her arrival, so that the wedding, after many days of waiting, will take place. The ceremony ends, and the beginning of a new lifestyle will begin. This is something completely different than has ever been experienced before. Love is everywhere, and there are no ugly or bad things happening—no sorrow, no crying, no death, no sin, no separation, no time, no limitations, no wants, no fear and no limitations as to time or space. Wow! What a day that will be!

The Father planned this from the beginning and now, throughout the church age, the bride is being made ready for the wedding in the sky. God the Father planned it, Christ the Son paid for it at Calvary's cross, and the Holy Spirit sealed it by indwelling our beings and empowering our lives. Keeping all of this in mind should be motivation enough to keep on loving our "first love" and to give us enough passion and courage to change the loveless, immoral dark world around us. Let us get busy. The wedding day may not be far away when we enter the land of beginning again.

When Paul wrote to the church in Rome, he clearly communicated what Christ thinks of same sex marriage and the new definition of the family. *"Therefore God delivered them over to degrading passions. For even their females exchanged natural sexual relations for unnatural ones. The males in the same way also left natural relations with females and males committed shameless acts with males and received in their own persons the appropriate penalty of their error."* (Romans 1:26-27).

Pastors and other church leaders need to remember that we are His bride, and while continuing to love and value each person we must take a firm stand and teach the generations following that this is not God's plan for the family. *"He created them male and female. When they were created He blessed them and called them 'man.'"* (Gen. 5:2).

Christ is still walking amidst our churches, and He will hold pastors and other church leaders in His right hand. If our culture is to be changed, it will take the strong stand of courageous leadership to do so. We must depend on the presence and power of the risen Christ to change the culture, or the culture will dictate and define who we are and what we are supposed to do.

Family as community is vital for the survival of each generation. One of the destructive issues is brought about by the failure of marriages. Children are being reared by single parents. This distorts the plan of authority set forth by God when the family was created. In many cases, young boys grow up without the role model of a father or husband. In some cases, other relatives, such as an uncle, step up to meet this need. Pastors and church leaders need to provide training opportunities for the youth on what God expects of a marriage. Churches can address this problem by recruiting foster families within their congregation to care for children forced out of their natural family.

Practical subjects need to be shared, such as the role of the husband and wife as father and mother, how authority works in the home, and why discipline is important and necessary. All of these should be lived out in an atmosphere of unconditional love. There are many practical things that can be done to strengthen the church's modeling of Christ's plan for the family.

In addition to the family, the church is another community that Christ wants to walk with. He can only do this as individual members open their lives up to Him and allow Him to be present. This is made possible by public worship and private devotion to Christ. It is made possible by yielding our human spirits to the indwelling Holy Spirit. He is the one that Jesus promised to the disciples in John 14:15-18: *"When the Counselor (Holy Spirit) comes, the One I will send to you from the Father, the Spirit of truth, who proceeds from the Father-He will testify about Me."* (John 15:26). *"Nevertheless I am telling you the truth. It is for your benefit that I go away, because if I don't go away the 'Counselor' will not come to you. When the Spirit of truth comes, he will guide you into all the truth. For He will not speak on his own but He will speak whatever He hears. He will also declare to you what is to come."* (John 16:7; 13).

The church is the body of Christ in the world today. Christ was limited with a self-imposed limitation while He was here on earth (Phil. 2:7). But when He ascended back to the Father, He sent us His Holy Spirit so that we could be His presence and power to meet the needs of others everywhere and glorify the Lord Jesus—the Head of the body the church.

Jesus said I am *"the one who holds the seven stars in his*

right hand. " (Rev. 2:1). Seven stars are the pastors of the seven churches. Christ holds both pastors and churches in His hand. *Hold* is a strong word. One construction of *hold* shows that only a part of the thing is gripped due to its size, a ball bat for instance. The other *hold* shows that the whole thing is gripped as a nut or coin. This is the picture portrayed here.

The risen Lord has a grip on the entire church and all His pastors. They are in His hand and the hand is cupped over them. If the church and pastor yield to the control of Christ, they can never go wrong. Our safety and security rests on this fact. *"I give unto them eternal life; and they shall never perish; neither shall any man pluck them out of my hand."* (John 10:28).

Commendation or Condemnation

Jesus is pictured as walking among His churches: *"I know your works and labor."* (Rev. 2:2). He knows what is going on. He is active in His churches. *"For where two or three are gathered together in my name, I am there among them."* (Matthew 18:20). He is in their midst and therefore knows all about the church. Since He knows all, He has a word of compliment, and a word of complaint.

He understands and compliments individuals for their labor. The word *labor* means one who works to sheer exhaustion. If we desire His presence and power, we must labor with fervency and zeal. He is the One who is hold-

17

ing us in His right hand. For each member of the community—every family, church, labor, and government—it is Christ's desire to enter, empower, and bless with His very presence. He places high value on what we do as well as who we are. He says to Ephesus, *"I know (oida - knowledge by observation) thy works."* [5] He understands and compliments the individuals for their labor. Again, the word labor means one who works to sheer exhaustion, and zeal.

The church at Ephesus had taken a stand against false doctrine and evil practice. They would not tolerate evil practices by their members. It takes courage on the part of believers to stand for right and truth, but Jesus commended the Ephesian Christians for confronting error in the lives of other believers.

There was a group of people in the Ephesian church who addressed themselves as Nicolaitans. Jesus said He hated this group (Rev. 2:6). The two words, *nikao* meaning "to conquer," and *laos* meaning "the people" or laity, form the root of the name Nicolaitans. The term was applied to those who originated the system that divided the church of Jesus Christ into two divisions, the clergy and the laity. There was no such distinction in the church's beginning and no Biblical basis for it today. Every believer is a believer-priest and does not need to go through anyone to get to God. *"Therefore, let us approach the throne of grace with boldness, so that we may receive mercy and find grace to help us at the proper time."* (Heb. 4:16). Jesus is our High

Priest and Head of the church, and we address our needs to Him directly and not through some intermediary.

Three times in the Scripture Jesus uses the word church (*ecclesia*) *as* "the called out ones." He used it when He solicited Peter's opinion on what people were saying about Him (Matt. 16:18). Then He asked Peter personally, "Who do you say that I am?" Peter responded, *Thou are the Christ, the Son of the living God.*" He told Peter that upon his confession of faith that He was the Messiah, "*I will build My church.*"

The other two times Jesus used this word was in relationship to discipline (Matt. 18:15). A thriving church community must maintain a loving and caring source of discipline which demands that believers be courageous in confronting error, especially in doctrine. Care must be exercised so as not to become judgmental and legalistic. James tells us, *"My brothers, if any among you strays from the truth, and someone turns him back, let him know that whoever turns a sinner from the error of his way will save a life from death and cover a multitude of sins."* (James 5:20). We must not only teach what we believe but also how we must behave. The book in the New Testament written by Paul to the church at Ephesus has three chapters on what to believe and three chapters on how to behave.

Many today invest in popular religious television ministries without knowing what doctrines they embrace. By using God-given resources for these, supporters are actually becoming part of promoting error instead of truth. It is wise to look into these ministries and see if they are operating within the boundaries of the truth as presented in the Word of God. A great need in these crucial days is for the believer to be a courageous leader in each area of life, home, church, and business. This can be accomplished by remembering that our "first love" with Jesus as our groom is to be the loving bride waiting for His return.

Promises

Our Lord gives a gracious promise in closing. "*To him that overcomes, I will give to eat of the tree of life, which is in the Paradise of God.*" (Rev. 2:7). Jesus is calling us back to the beginning. He calls us back when life first began. Remember the darkness that was over everything when God turned on the lights.

Application

In that first Paradise, Eden, He placed all kinds of trees for man to enjoy. He put a restriction on one tree—the tree of the knowledge of good and evil. So now His promise to the overcomer is that there will be no restrictions. There is freedom from every hindrance to happiness. Mankind does not have to fight the darkness of the world any more, for he is living in the Light of the Blessed Redeemer. No sun is needed to light the day or moon to light the night, for Jesus is the Light. Notice the wonderful gifts that are present: life everlasting—eternal, with no more death, light with no more darkness, and love—with no more anger and hate. This is what Jesus came to give us. To restore the power and mighty presence of Jesus we must repent if we have left our first love, We must remember what price was paid for our Paradise experience, and we must renew our unconditional love for our Lord.

God created us with a body—a house to live in—and breathed into us our living soul that is eternal. The soul is made up of a mind to think and retain knowledge with, a will to make decisions and choices with, and emotions enabling us to love, hate, desire, grieve, rejoice, and more. He then breathed into this house with the soul the "breath of life." That breath of life—the human spirit—in our forefather Adam was the vital link between the Creator and His creature.

When the first couple disobeyed God, that vital link was severed. However, our loving Father made a way for it to be restored. He provided a Redeemer—a Savior, who is Christ our Lord. When we repent of our sin and place our trust in Christ and His death and resurrection, for us that link is restored. Jesus sends the Holy Spirit to live inside us and to be our Counselor. Yielding to the Spirit and following His leading will help us rediscover our "first love."

STUDY GUIDE

F- Forgetting your first love is serious business. How would you go about recovering your first love for Jesus?

A- All things work together for good to those who love the Lord. How have you seen this truth work in your life?

I- *"I know your works. . ."* These are Jesus' words to this church. He knew all about the good things they were doing. How does this truth make you feel?

T- *"To him who overcomes, I will give to eat of the tree of life . . ."* What do these words mean to you?

H- *"Hear what the Spirit says to the churches."* What do you hear the Holy Spirit saying to you in this letter?

Chapter 2

ADDRESSING ADVERSITY

~

The Church at Smyrna
(Revelation 2:8-11)

<u>Introduction</u>

It was 103 degrees in Knoxville, Tennessee on September 5, 1954. The preparation for this day began on February 14th when the groom asked the bride to be his wife.

The day came, and the couple pledged their love and loyalty to each other. The Pastor prayed over the young couple, and friends and family celebrated the occasion. This was a happy day. But the days following were not filled with happiness. There were sad times in the home going of parents, disappointments in the lives of children, personal illness, and struggles to make financial ends meet. But in the midst of all of this were faith, hope, patience, and love that pulled them through.

To the followers of Jesus, the crucifixion seemed to end it all. The eleven that were closest to Him, with the exception of John, forsook Him and fled. But on that first Easter morning it all changed when He appeared to the women and later to the eleven in the Upper Room (Luke 24:36).

The two followers walking on the road to Emmaus help us to understand the tenor of the day. As Jesus spoke to them, and they did not recognize Him, they said that their religious leaders had delivered Him up to be crucified and *"we hoped that it had been He who should have redeemed Israel."* (Luke 24:21). A few moments later, Jesus preached a great sermon from His Bible—the Old Testament—Moses and the Law, the Prophets and the Psalms. He indicated that He would pass on by their home, but they persuaded Him to join them. As He broke the bread and blessed it, they came to understand who He was, and their hope sprang alive (Luke 24:30).

Just a few days before, when He was in the Upper Room with the disciples He had "broken bread and blessed it." (Luke 22:19). Then He gave it to the disciples and explained that this was His body that would be sacrificed for mankind's sin. When the Emmaus followers ran back the seven miles to Jerusalem and found the disciples in the Upper Room, they recounted their experience and said, *"And they told what things were done along the way, and how he was known by them in the "breaking of bread."* (Luke 24:35). Knowing that Jesus had died, was buried, and this was the third day and He was alive, hope was resurrected. What they had hoped for had now become a reality. The breaking of bread would foreshadow His becoming "broken" on the cross to heal the brokenness in the lives of the whole human family. *"Yet He Himself bore our sicknesses, and He carried our pains; but we in turn regarded Him stricken, struck down by God, and afflicted. But He was pierced because of our transgressions, crushed because of our iniquities; punishment for our peace was on Him and we are healed by His wounds. We all went astray like sheep; we all have turned to our own way; and the Lord has punished Him for the iniquity of us all."* (Isa. 53:4-6).

<u>History</u>

The church in Smyrna was under heavy affliction.[6] Afflictions are sometimes sent by God to instruct and help us grow in our faith. They are brought on at other times by satanic forces. At other times we bring them on ourselves. But as certain as they come, they will also come to an end. The prophet Nahum said about afflictions from God, *"Though I have afflicted thee, I will afflict thee no more."* (Nahum 1:12b). It is not hard for our Lord to turn night into day.

The Church Overseer

Polycarp was the bishop of the Smyrna church.[7] We do not know how the church started. It was located about 35 miles north of Ephesus where Paul spent 3-plus years. John introduced Polycarp to the Christian faith and later installed him as the overseer of the Smyrna church.

This city was founded as a Greek colony on the "Hill of Pagus" in 1000 B.C. It was later completely destroyed in 600 B.C. One of the generals of Alexander the Great rebuilt the city in 301-251 B.C.

A Beautiful City

It was a beautiful city. Unlike many of the cities that developed without purpose and forethought, the city planners of Smyrna had obviously done their homework. There was cohesiveness and a pattern about the architecture that made it blend together, and as one stood at the sea harbor looking up toward the top of Mount Pagus, he could see a panorama that led it to be called "a crown." [8]

The Spice of Myrrh

The city is alive today and is known as Izmir in modern Turkey. Smyrna drew its name and popularity from the spice of myrrh. This spice was made from the juice of a thorny plant. It was crushed in order to extract this special spice that had multiple usages. A primary use was in embalming. We recall that the wise men brought three gifts to the baby Jesus—gold, frankincense and myrrh. At His crucifixion, they offered myrrh mixed with vinegar to help Him deal with the pain, but He refused. Again, when two of His followers, Joseph of Arimathea and Nicodemus, came to prepare His body for burial they brought about a 100-pound weight mixture of spices, myrrh, and aloes (John 19:39).

It is interesting to note that the prophet Isaiah, looking to the second coming of the Lord Jesus, mentions gold and frankincense, but no myrrh. This prophecy of the return of Christ for His church is referred to as "the blessed hope." Myrrh was associated with death, and when the Lord returns there will be no more death.

Era of Persecution

The church at Smyrna represents the era of church history when persecution was the order of the day.[9] It represents the church age of persecution and martyrdom from the apostolic period to 325A.D. This was the time when Christians were thrown to the lions, they fought in the Roman arena, and were hidden in the catacombs.

The church had to deal with the destruction of the city in their history. They had to deal with the Roman government that was promoting Caesar worship. In addition, they had to deal with the Jews who were seeking to stamp out Christianity. Like the thorny plant that was crushed to give up the myrrh, the Christians at Smyrna were being crushed by the weight of all this adversity.

Attribute

Our Lord steps in at this time and reveals another of His attributes. He says, *"I am the first and the last, the one who was dead and came to life."* (Rev.2:8). Then He tells the church He knows what is going on.

"I know your tribulation, affliction and poverty." (vs. 9).

When affliction and adversity come upon us, it is good to know that someone knows about this and cares. Affliction wears many different suits. There is the affliction that comes in broken relationships. This is certainly true in family circles. When the basic unit of society breaks down there is pain; there is discomfort. Physical affliction produces its own set of problems. Pain is generally associated with physical ailments. Physical limitations are imposed by some foreign agent that invades the body and seeks its destruction, or at least the impairment of its normal function. Financial affliction can cause many a sleepless night when the lack of resources dwindle, forcing poverty. Affliction may arise in the work place with demands made upon employees by their superiors that create a hostile work atmosphere. In times like these, hope can easily be lost.

Jesus reveals Himself to the church in Smyrna as the one who was dead and now is alive. He tells the church *"I know your hurts."* (Rev. 2:9). He is offering both sympathy and empathy. Sympathy says, I know how you feel. Empathy says, I *feel* what you feel. When Jesus said, *"I am He that was dead but now I am alive,"* He was referring to the resurrection. All hope was lost when Jesus' body was taken down from the cross and placed in the borrowed tomb of Joseph of Arimitheia. But before the first rays of sun cast their brightness upon the garden tomb, the believers found it was empty, and hope began to spring alive.

These words brought encouragement and hope to

the hurting, disappointed group of people in Smyrna. They were under tremendous pressure, and the one thing they needed was reassurance and hope. The Greek word for hope is *elpis,* and it is simply a favorable and confident expectation. So the hope for every believer is based upon the fact that Christ arose on the third day, having defeated death, Hell, and the grave. He has given to us a favorable and confident expectation that *"death is swallowed up in victory, O death where is thy sting, O grave where is thy victory?"* (1 Cor. 15:55).

Many circumstances can render us with an attitude of hopelessness: the breakup of a family relationship, a debilitating illness, loss of financial resources, loss of confidence in friends, and disappointment in church leadership. All can render us without hope. All of these and more seek to destroy our faith and our joy. What is needed to address each of these and more is hope—favorable and confident expectation.

The greatest enemy that seeks to destroy our hope is fear. Jesus often used two words to instill hope in his followers: *"Fear not."* Someone has said that there are at least 365 statements from our Lord like, *"fear not; be not afraid,"* one for every day of the year. Jesus said, *"You will have suffering in this world. Be encouraged I have overcome the world."* (John 16:33).

The Christian life today, if lived according to the Word of God, will experience persecution and adversaries. Recently 21 Christians from the Coptic Church in Egypt were killed for their faith in Jesus Christ. Pointing his gun at her, a high school student in Colorado asked a young student if she was a Christian. She acknowledged that she was, and he pulled the trigger. A church built a mission building in an ethnic community different than the mother church. Routinely the windows were broken out by youth from another religion, throwing rocks.

Smyrna was where emperor worship began. The city, like many other Asian towns, was happy to be subject to Rome. Rome provided protection from invaders, built roads, developed harbors, and set forth a set of laws that brought a form of justice to the land. So when the time came to extract loyalty from the people, they were asked to burn a pinch of incense and state, "Caesar is lord." The faithful Christians refused to do this, which resulted in a loss of job opportunities, ostracization by the citizens, and refusals of every kind. So the faithful people of Smyrna suffered and became not only afflicted, but impoverished as well.[10]

Condemnation or Commendation

In essence, the Lord said, I know about this and I have come to bring you hope and encouragement. I not only died and now am alive, but I am the first and the last and everything in between. Often Jesus said He was the Alpha and the Omega—the first and last letters of the Greek alphabet. He is the first and the last and everything in between. If you take the entire Greek alphabet, you can spell out any need you have, and Christ is there to meet that need. He is the blessed hope.

There were three words that Jesus used to describe their affliction. He said He knew their *tribulation*, or affliction. [11] This word describes a form of punishment used by placing a heavy rock on a person's chest and squeezing the very life out of the individual over a period of time. He uses the word *poverty*. This word describes the man who works for a living just to get by. Professing Christians who owned businesses would have to shut down because no one would buy from them. Others would not hire the Christian for fear of reprisal. Finally, He uses the word *blasphemes*, which implies slander.

<u>Promise</u>

Jesus gave them two things to do to continue in hope. *"Fear not"* and *"Be thou faithful unto death and I will give you the crown of life."* (Rev. 2:10). Remember, Smyrna sat on a hill, and when you stood at the sea looking up it had the appearance of a crown. Jesus in essence said, "Don't be afraid; just be faithful, and I will give you the "crown of life." There was another hill that they should remember—the hill of Calvary. It was there that Christ made a way for every person to have hope that would dispel every fear. Jesus said, *"Don't fear those that kill the body but are not able to kill the soul. Rather, fear Him who is able to destroy both soul and body in hell."* (Matt. 10:28).

<u>Application</u>

Jesus tells them that He knows their *tribulation*.[12] This word is used to describe the scars left by the Roman whip. However, Jesus used it in the sense to describe the stones that grind the wheat, and He remained the giver of love and compassion who would stand by them though it all. He also said He knew their poverty. Their persecution had caused them to lose their trade and their social standing; they had lost it all. But they still had Jesus. In the adversity they faced they overlooked Him, and since many of them faced death in the persecution Jesus tells them that He was once dead (His body), but He is alive forevermore. This brought life to those persecuted saints. How are you being persecuted? Hope is what is needed and must be expressed. He tells me that death only sets free the limitations. "Do not fear the body, but the soul, for that is the *you* that will live forever either in Heaven or in Hell." Today you may be trapped with addictions, heroin, methamphetamines, alcohol, and marijuana. In addition, many have given up loved ones in death, and they grieve not knowing how they will make it emotionally or financially. Others are faced with some debilitating disease, and others are faced with the breakup of the family. Hope is needed with each of these trials.

When adversity strikes, the tendency is to ask, "Why me, Lord?" Or just walk away from your "first love" for the Lord Jesus. Please remember that Christ walked away from the tomb on that first Easter morning, thus declaring that men may kill the body but the real you that lives inside your body will never die. Each person born out of time will live forever, either in Heaven with Christ as a believer, or with Satan in Hell. His hope helps us not to be ashamed. If you are faced with adversity today, the best thing you can do is to turn back to Jesus, your first love, and remember that all the hope we have came alive on that first Easter morning. He says, *"I know"* and He does; He has your address. Find someone today who is struggling with adversity. You will not have to go very far. Find some way to help restore hope in their life.

STUDY GUIDE

F- First. When Jesus tells this church that He is First, what does this mean to you?

A- *"The angel of the church."* Who is this? Why address the letter to the angel of the church?

I- *"I will give you the crown of life."* What does this promise mean to you? How can you gain this crown?

T- Tribulation is mentioned two times in this letter. What does this mean each time?

H- Hope. Hope is found in the resurrection of Jesus Christ. How does this give you hope as you live your daily life?

Chapter 3

SHARPENING THE SWORD

~

The Church at Pergamum
(Revelation 2:12-17)

Introduction

The chief dividing line between believers over the Scriptures centers around how each group views the Word of God. Is it our full and complete authority, or do we need to add historical tradition to this authority? Is it reliable and relative to the present generation? Does it have answers to the present problems being experienced in our culture? Which translation is reliable? Has the translation included the most recent findings from recently discovered ancient manuscripts?

The first exposure I had to the Bible was in a small rural church, New Hope Missionary Baptist, in the western area of our state. It was located about 3 miles from our farm. On Sundays, I would go with my family to this church and was a member of the "card" class. Our little class of preschoolers sat on a bench and was given a card with a picture on one side and a verse of Scripture on the other. We were given the reward of a piece of candy if we could recite the Scripture by the next Sunday.

In our home we had a large family Bible with all our ancestors' names written in the front. I also recall with great delight visiting my grandparents and watching my grandfather read the Bible to himself by the light of a kerosene lamp.

When I graduated from high school, my parents gave me my first copy of the Word of God with my name engraved on the front in gold letters. I cherished this and took it with me throughout my college years. Unfortunately, I did not read it on a daily basis but took it with me to church on Sundays.

My early Bible teachers taught that this book would tell me how to live right in the sight of God, and if I failed to follow the rules, this would result in the judgment of God on my life. From all of this I developed a healthy respect for God and the Bible—the Word of God.

John has been recording the vision Christ has given him about the seven churches in Asia. Each of these churches faced various problems within and without. The problems they faced were addressed by the risen, glorified

Christ who was seen walking among the churches and holding the church leadership up by His right hand (Rev. 1:12-16). The problem each church faced revealed a specific period in the history of Christianity. First, Ephesus represents the Apostolic age. Next, Smyrna represents the era of severe persecution following the Apostolic age to 325 A.D. Now consider the church at Pergamum and the problems they faced during the period when the church was married to the world—325 A.D.-600 A.D.

Attribute

The attribute revealed by Christ to this church was described as: *"The One that has the sharp, two-edged sword."* (Rev 2:12). This is a clear reference to the Word of God. *"For the Word of God is living and effective and sharper than any two-edged sword, penetrating as far as the separation of soul and spirit, joints and marrow. It is able to judge the ideas and thoughts of the heart."* (Heb. 4:12).

The present generation and culture has largely laid this aside as reflected in the redefining of the basic unit of humanity—the family. The Word of God is clear on this subject for it clearly states, *"On the day that God created man, He made him in the likeness of God: He created them male and female. When they were created, He blessed them and called them man."* (Gen.5:1-2). The word *man* at the end of this statement as used here is to refer to humanity. Previously, God had laid down the definition of a family: *"This is why a man leaves his father and mother and bonds with his wife, and they become one flesh."* (Gen. 2:24).

In America, on an annual basis there are more divorces than there are marriages. The strong push by the homosexual community to gain recognition, prominence, and acceptance is in direct conflict with the authority of the Word of God. (Rom 1:19-32 HCSB).

The common practice of premarital sexual immorality, sometimes with multiple partners, destroys the godly plan for the establishment of the family, bringing shame, guilt, and destructive doubts. This immorality was never meant to be a factor in the formation of the family. Add to this the conception of an unwanted pregnancy possibly ending in abortion and leaving a scar on the souls of the couple, depriving them of the joy that should have been. God can and will forgive and cover this wrong, but the scar left in the lives of these individuals will always be there (I John 1:9).

The tragedy of our culture is that what once sneaked down the back alleys of our nation now parades down Broadway. In addition, there is the evil of human trafficking with young women as young as 12 being lured and trapped in a lifestyle of prostitution. The church needs to address these issues and offer solutions, not condemnation.

The slaughter of innocent children through abortion—as many as 125,000 a year—is a fatal disrespect for human life that was created by God. God loves and takes joy in His creation. He said about the creation of mankind: *"God saw all that he made and it was very good."* (Gen. 1:31).

History

The city of Pergamum sat on a huge rocky hill with the beautiful Aegean Sea just 15 miles away.[13] Smyrna was 49 miles away and Thyatira 36 miles. The Caucus River flowed nearby, and may have served as the region's border between Mysia and Lydia.

Pergamum was a great cultural center with an outstanding library that was started by Plutarch, the Greek historian. This library grew to over 200,000 volumes (scrolls), and was second only to the library in Alexandria. Most of these scrolls were made out of papyrus from Egypt. When this source was exhausted, they developed an alternative material made from the skin of goats and sheep. Today, most universities give degrees made from this same type of material, called vellum.

The most impressive sight as one approached the city was the altar to Zeus. It was 90 feet high, 115 feet wide, and 110 feet deep in dimension. It has been rebuilt and is now located in the Staafliche museum in Berlin, Germany. The style of sculpture on the altar is different from that found in the Parthenon in Athens. This sculpture has gods fighting, waving, and running—all very physical. You could get excited just standing before it.

<u>Commendation and Condemnation</u>

The risen and glorified Christ says some good things about this church and then one bad. He tells them He knows their location—*"where you live–where Satan has his throne"*—in the town where people from all over the world came to offer evil sacrifices to Zeus Sater (Savior) (Rev. 2:13). It could have been written: "And you live where the god of healing, Askeplos, has a temple." He had become so famous that they called him Savior, Askleplos sotar. This was offensive to the Christians. But they were faithful in the culture by holding on to the name of Christ and in spite of the evil culture did not deny their faith even in the days of Antipas "My faithful witness" (Rev.2:13). The word for witness and martyr are the same. Twice (Rev. 1:5; 3:14), he is called the faithful witness. The name Antipas is only found here. His name means *anti*–against, *pas*–all. He stood against all the evil surrounding him. He was faithful and true in the very place where "Satan lives" (Rev.2:13). He was killed for his faithfulness and opposition to all these evil practices.

Are we willing to stand firm on the two-edged sword of the Word of God, even if it means giving up our lives. The recent video of 12 individuals, blindfolded and kneeling before their executioner, knowing within minutes their heads would be severed from their bodies, is quite alarming. This is happening in our world as we come to the close of the year 2015.

Some theologians explain that Satan had set up his government in Babylon, but when he saw the handwriting of God on the wall (Dan. 5:5), he moved his government to Pergamum. So Antipas stood for Christ in a sin-infested, Satan-controlled culture. Jesus commended his memory for this.[14]

How would you like to be remembered? Would you be willing to give up your physical life to stand against the satanic influence in our culture?

Now Jesus tells them their "bad." There are two things He named. First, he said they were holding to the teaching of Balaam (Num. 22-29). When you read this story, Balaam was hired as a false prophet by the King of Moab to help defeat the people of God. God turned Balaam's curses into blessings, so he devised another way, and that was to get their men involved with strange women. So the "bad" of the Christians at Pergamum was that they compromised and exchanged purity for pleasure.

Compromising Christianity is the rule of the day in our culture and our churches. Churches have become so focused on becoming a "seeker-friendly church" that we have forgotten that the gospel is good news, but good news has to be set against the background of "bad news." We hear in John 3:17 that *"God did not send his Son into the world to condemn the world, but that the world might be saved through him."* The next verse is usually left out, *"Anyone who believes in Him is not condemned, but anyone who does not believe is already condemned, because he has*

41

not believed in the name of the one and only Son of God." (John 3:18).

The second "bad" that Jesus notes is that there are those who are teaching the doctrine of the Nicolaitans. Jesus had spoken to the church at Ephesus and commended them for hating the doctrine of the Nicolaitans, which Jesus said, "I hate." (Rev. 2:6). The word comes from two Greek words, *nikao*, to conquer, and *laos*, the people. This was the beginning of setting up a structure of clergy versus laity. Those who held this doctrine placed authority in the clergy and lifted that above the laity. This doctrine taught that the clergy alone got their words from God. But Scripture teaches that the bride that Jesus came and died for, He came to set free (John 8:32; 8:36). *"If the Son makes you free, ye shall be free indeed."* (Gal. 3:26-29).

There is only one High Priest that is over all of creation and all creatures—the Lord Jesus Christ. In the church, the bride of Christ, all are priests and constitute the priesthood of believers. All stand on equal ground in regard to authority. Churches may, according to Scripture, have elders/pastors and deacons. These are servant roles and receive their authority from the local body of believers.

The book we call the Bible contains 39 books in the Old Testament or Old Covenant and 27 in the New. These books were written over a period of 1400 years by at least 40 different writers. Yet it all fits nicely together to tell the story of the creation and fall of the human race. It tells of the promise of a Savior and the fulfilling of the promise by the death, burial, resurrection, and ascension of Jesus leading to the establishment of the body of Christ—the church—His bride.

Promise

Christ makes a threefold promise to the church at Pergamum: He will feed them on hidden manna and He will give them a white stone and write a new name on it. According to Patterson, "So the promises for the overcomer at Pergamum include sustenance with heavenly manna, holiness indicated by acquittal and recognized by a white stone, and a certain intimacy, a new name, given by the authority of Christ Himself to the individual believer."[15]

Application

The white stone with a new name written on it has various meanings and applications. To the overcomer, *"I will give him a white stone and upon the stone a new name written, which no one knoweth but he that received it."* (Rev. 2:17). There have been in the Christian literature several explanations as to what this means. Each of them has relevancy and application for today.

The white stone was given to a person who after trial was justly acquitted, and with the white stone could never be tried again, being free from condemnation. The white stone was given to a man to denote he was a "free" man of the city. It established his citizenship as a free citizen. The white stone was given to a soldier as a reward for victories won in a battle.[16]

The last discovery of the gift of the white stone has to do also with the new name. This stone was known as the *tessara hospitalis*. Two men who were friends, about to part, would divide a white stone into two, each carrying with him half, upon which was inscribed the name of the other friend. It may be that stone in each case would be bequeathed to a son, and sometimes generations after, a man would meet another, and they would find they possessed the complementary halves of one white stone. Their friendship would at once be created upon the basis of a friendship made long ago.

This white stone given by Jesus has a wonderful application to the Christian life. Before receiving Christ as our Savior, we are under condemnation as sinners. Once we receive Christ as Savior and Lord, we are justified. This means we are free citizens of the family of God with all the rights and privileges of Kingdom citizenship. In addition, we have fought a good fight and are now victors returning from battle. We are rewarded for our courage and faithfulness. Finally, if we have found a friend in Jesus, we have the other half of the stone to match His, and our fellowship with the Master is forever.

The church at Pergamum is encouraged to "hold on" to the truth—the Amen—the Word of God. While the Bible is a best seller, it is perhaps the least read. Today, false prophets still seek to persuade God's people to compromise their belief and faith in the infallible Word of God. Heresy reeks from some of the institutions of higher education. Nearly all the Ivy League schools were started with a strong belief in the Word of God and commitment to seeing lives changed by the preaching and teaching of the Scriptures. Today all of that has changed.

The Ten Commandments handed down to Moses as God's law are being broken twenty-four/seven. At the head of the list of idolatries are sports. In a nation that seeks to cope with poverty, hunger, and neglect, billions of dollars are spent annually on sports. Sports are not evil, but expending billions of dollars desperately needed by the disadvantaged of our world on coaches and players is wrong. This has become America's number one idol.

In addition, huge corporations expend millions to see who can pay their chief executive more. The Word of God says, *"Thou shall not covet."* (Exodus 20:17). Greed is seeking assets beyond God's provision. The same Word says, *"Thou shall not kill"* (vs. 13), yet our nation has legalized abortion—the taking of innocent life. How long do we think that a righteous Holy God will tolerate a nation that grossly and flagrantly violates the commandments (rules) that He gave as a safeguard for all His creation?

Today we are a nation living in fear. A terrorist act in California that took the lives of innocent people was just one of several violent acts that has happened recently. The nation living in fear closed down a large school in California after a threat had been received. Videos made by a false religious group, of Christians about to be beheaded by their captors because they would not bow to a false god, were frightening. This is a call for America to wake up to the Word of God. He that hath ears, let him hear what the Spirit is saying to the Light (the church) that needs to shine brighter now than ever before.

Do you have ears? What action will you take to change the culture of your generation and bring it in line with the Sharp, Two-Edged Sword? What is your church doing to engage the enemy? The enemy is described in Ephesians 6:10-17. Paul also tells the Christian what to use as battle gear. Is the Word of God being taught in your church? Does your church hold to the doctrine of the Nicolaitans? Does your church elevate clergy above laity? What is your church doing to prepare the youth for making wise choices as to choosing a life partner? Are you serving as a mentor to anyone? Have you compromised your witness when you have felt that it might offend someone?

These are some hard questions to deal with. The measuring stick is the Word of God. It is relevant for every generation. It is the Truth spelled out for the entire world to see, believe, and live. It is the book to live by, and it is the book to die by.

The church of Jesus Christ must not tolerate within her borders those who lower the standard of truth's requirements. God's order is the order of peace, but it is always peace based upon purity, for the wisdom that is from above is first pure, and then peaceable (James 3:17).

STUDY GUIDE

F- Fast. Jesus said this church at Pergamum held fast to His name. What does this mean, and how can you do this?

A- Against. Jesus mentioned that He had a few things against this church. What were they, and can you think of anything He might have against you?

I- *"I will come against them with the 'sword of My mouth.'"* What is this sword? Can you use the same sword against your enemy—Satan? How?

T- The white stone. What is this white stone and the new name written on it?

H- Hidden manna. What is this hidden manna? How can you eat of it?

Chapter 4

PURPOSEFUL PROGRESS

~

The Church at Thyatira
(Revelation 2:18-29)

<u>Introduction</u>

A few years ago there was a television show under the title, "I led three lives." An undercover agent for the FBI lived in a bedroom community of the nation's capital. He went to work like other men on a daily basis. He performed his job at work like his peers, but outside of work he hung out with some seedy characters that were always plotting crimes. He really was a different man to each crowd, at home, at the office, and after work.

John tells us in I John 1:15 that "*God is light and there is absolutely no darkness in Him.*" If we are perfectly honest, there is a dark side to each of our lives. While the light of

Christ is in us, at times we shade the light where others cannot see the darkness we cling to.

In more recent days, there is a TV series called *Undercover Boss*. This is where the boss of a business goes undercover and works alongside his employees. He gets to hear, see, and feel what they are thinking and saying on a daily basis. He sees firsthand the dark side in respect to their work.

The attribute and character Jesus displays for the church in Thyatira is one in which He looks and sees with piercing fiery eyes. Those flaming, fiery eyes penetrate the thickest darkness in our souls. He looks and sees today the area of darkness in our life's walk just as He did for the members of the church at Thyatira.

As the sun arose Sabbath day over the city of Philippi in Macedonia, Paul and Silas searched for a scenic place to engage in prayer. They had come to Macedonia due to a call from the Holy Spirit, *"Cross over to Macedonia and help us."* (Acts 16:9). Paul was no stranger to meeting others. That day he met a lady named Lydia from Thyatira. She told Paul that she belonged to one of the many trade guilds (unions) in Thyatira. These trade guilds represented many of the industries, and Lydia's was the dyeing industry. She had come to market her goods in Philippi. She told Paul that she was a "seller of purple." Thyatira was famous for a particular purple dye that was extracted from the neck of a mollusk. This mollusk, when crushed, gave up this purple fluid, and when struck by air produced a beautiful crimson color. In addition, the water in Thyatira had a certain quality to it that enhanced the dye to keep it from fading.

Lydia, who was a worshiper of God, heard Paul and Silas praying, and the Lord opened her heart to the gospel, and she was converted and baptized (Acts 16:14-33).

There is no written statement on how the church got started in Thyatira, but it is not unlikely that Lydia returned to her home and witnessed of her faith in Jesus Christ. The account in Acts 16:15 tells us that other members of her family were baptized with her. Lydia was the first recorded convert in Europe.

History

Jesus addressed the church as the Son of God (Rev.2:18). Since each of the churches addressed by Jesus represents a certain prophetic period of church history, Thyatira represents the period known as the *Dark Ages*—600 A.D. -1500 A.D. [17]

A time of spiritual wickedness and gross darkness existed during this period. The world saw a rapid rise of Romanism that expressed its power and made changes that took away the freedom of the individual believer. The direction of Romanism focused on making Jesus the son of Mary, naming her the Queen of Heaven. As Jesus expresses Himself as the Son of God, He sets the record straight, not allowing Himself to be degraded simply as the son of a human mother. He announces to the entire world that He alone is the Son of God with a human mother but a Heavenly Father (vs. 18).

While it was truly prophesied that *"a virgin shall conceive and bear a son"* (Isa.7:14), it is equally true that the Son was given by the Father before Jesus was ever born of Mary (Isa.9:6). There is the teaching that if one wishes to be heard in the Heavenly court, then you must reach the Father by praying through Mary. This fallacy is nowhere to be found in the Scriptures.

__Attribute__

Now Jesus continues to reveal Himself as the one who has *"eyes of flaming fire"* with feet of *"fine bronze."* (Rev. 2:18). Bronze is made from a mixture of zinc and copper. It has great strength. Jesus wanted the church to know that He could see everything and had the strength to deal with it. There is nothing in the darkness of life that He does not know about. There was nothing in the church of Thyatira for which He did not have knowledge: *"The eyes of the Lord run to and fro throughout the whole earth, to show himself strong to the upright in heart." The eyes of the Lord thy God is always upon it from the beginning of the year to the end of the same."* (Deut. 11:12).

One day my mother took an American one-dollar bill and showed me an eyeball at the top of a pyramid. She said, "Son, you see this eye? God is the "all-seeing eye.""

He sees everything you do. As a small child, I literally thought that this big eyeball followed me around everywhere and, as such, knew and saw everything I did.

One of the good things Jesus saw in the church was the progress they were making. He said, *"Your last works are greater than the first."* (Rev.3:19). They had learned that the Christian experience was one of change. In many of Paul's writings, he speaks to this principle. To the church at Corinth, he said they were still just babies in their Christian growth. He said they could not take the strong meat of the Word of God but had to rely on milk. A person becomes a Christian by inviting Christ into their life (Rom. 10:9-10). That is when it all begins. Unfortunately for many new Christians, they spend years at this particular level. If you ask for their testimony, they will tell about their conversion and not much else. The lack of a strong discipleship ministry in the church leads the church to be filled with baby Christians. It is no wonder that these churches are always having conflict within the membership. Babies cry a lot, babies are selfish, babies need a lot of attention, and the list goes on. The church is the body of Christ, and it is necessary that it continue to grow in Christ-likeness. A strong evidence of progress and growth is to see the fruit of the Spirit being magnified in the membership (Gal. 5:22-23).

One of the ways a church can stay healthy is to have a mentoring program for new members. This is where a mature Christian will align with a new Christian and teach the spiritual disciplines of prayer, spiritual leadership, the Word of God, stewardship, and how these apply to daily living.

The flaming, piercing eyes of Jesus saw and knew what was going on in the church at Thyatira. He saw some good things, and He commended the church for them. He saw their works, faithfulness, service, and endurance. He also observed that they were making progress in those areas. But these flaming eyes went beyond the surface to see the wickedness that was being promoted and tolerated within the church by a false prophetess named Jezebel.

This was a well-known story to the church as told in I Kings 16:31. Jezebel was the daughter of Ethbaal, king of Sidon. She married Ahab, a wicked king of Israel, and introduced the worship of Baal to the nation Israel. This so-called prophetess was teaching the people of Israel that it was appropriate to eat meat offered to idols. This was strictly forbidden to the Israelites by God. The reason for this was the fact that in so doing they were approving the worship of a false god. The first commandment in the law was *"thou shall have no other gods before me."* (Ex. 20:3). Coupled with this wrong was the teaching that sexual immorality was to be practiced as an act of worship.

Commendation and Condemnation

While all of this was going on, the church turned their minds and hearts away from the truth and tolerated the false teaching and practices. However, there were a number—a remnant—which did not participate (Rev.2:24). They were encouraged to hold onto the truth. Jesus reminded the church that His feet were made of polished brass representing strength; He had the power and strength to see them through.

The urge today is to move up the ladder by selling our souls to corporations while forgetting our Creator and Master, who is the God of pardon and peace.

The nightly news on all three major networks spent at least 60% of their airtime reporting shootings, robberies, drug busts, child abuse and molestation, and other forms of violence in a recent telecast. It causes one to ask, "Did anyone in the capitol city of our state do anything good today?" The appropriate question to ask is why is all of this happening? Could it be that we have yielded to the spirits of toleration, compromise, political correctness, and the Jezebel of our culture. This wicked queen is wrecking the lives of our children, destroying the good family life, impairing the physical health of our bodies, and driving a whole generation to fear and anxiety attacks like we have never seen before.

Growing up on a farm before the days of GPS systems, there were other means to keep the rows straight. First, you develop a path by lining up two objects, one on the side of the field nearest you and another on the opposite side of the field. There is one conclusion to draw from this. If the first line is not straight, all the rest will follow the pattern.

Promises

Jesus instructs the church to "hold on until He comes." (Rev. 2:25). He is coming back to receive His bride (I Thess.4: 13-18). You may ask, as did some in the New Testament era, when is He coming back? We are the creatures of time; Jesus is in eternity where no time or space exists. *"One day with the Lord is as a thousand years."* (II Peter 3:8). If that is true, then Jesus has been gone two days. Jesus promised the early disciples that He was going away, but He assured them of His return" (John 14:1). He told them in this promise that it was necessary for Him to go away, for if He did not do so the Holy Spirit would not come. Fifty days after making this promise in an upper room in Jerusalem, the Holy Spirit descended upon 120 followers of Jesus. A few days later, literally thousands came to believe and receive Christ as Savior and Lord. Jesus always keeps His word. He also promised to give "authority over the nations." (Rev. 2:26). He then adds that He is "The Bright and Morning Star." (Rev. 2:28, 22:16). He is counseling the believer to not latch onto anything "new." When God spoke His word, in Genesis to tell us how it all began, and then in the Revelation how it all will end, it was done, finished, complete and needs nothing new added to it. Beware, He says, of those who come with something "new." Now He gives a solemn authority to the faithful believer, and as the darkness of night has appeared it will also disappear with the rising of the Bright and Morning star.

<u>Application</u>

The question we need to ask in this crazy upside down world is whose pattern are we going to follow, and how much will we bend to accommodate the culture? Am I going to bow before the Jezebels of today and get into sexual immorality or compromise with the controlled substance crowd to dull my senses by the new thrills and chills? Or, just cheat a little on my expense account? Or, finally pull off the big one by diverting funds to my benefit? How much tolerance will I allow in my life? The blazing eyes of the Lord see all of this, and His loving heart is strong as burnished brass to stand and help us. The Lord Jesus Christ is the answer; let's be sure we ask the right question.

STUDY GUIDE

F- Flame of fire. These words describe the eyes of Jesus. What does this suggest about Him, and how does this relate to you?

A- Allow. What were the things this church allowed that displeased Jesus?

I- *"I gave her time to repent."* Who was Jezebel, and what repentance did she need? How would you define repentance?

T- Thyatira. What do you know about the city of Thyatira? Are there any similarities to cities you know about today?

H- Hold fast. What did Jesus want this church to hold fast? How can you hold fast to that which pleases Him?

Chapter 5

THE WALKING DEAD
~
The Church at Sardis
(Revelation 3:1-6)

Introduction

Two friends seeking to keep themselves in good physical shape walked five days a week at the local Galleria Mall. Since they traveled separately, they used the parking lot to warm up before entering the mall to do their walk. While walking in the parking lot they would often find loose change that shoppers had evidently pulled out of their pockets when they secured their car keys. On one morning, the walker noticed a wristwatch lying on the ground. He picked it up and noticed that it was a Patek Philippe.

The watch had a peculiar self-winding mechanism. He did some computer research and learned that this was a very expensive watch priced at $16,000. He was elated, but his elation was short lived. He did not know what to do with the watch. Had it been stolen from a local jeweler? Did someone pay that kind of a price and then lose the watch? Had the watch been taken in a holdup or drug deal? This was really a mystery.

A few weeks passed, and he read an advertisement that a dealer was coming to purchase rare coins and expensive watches. The finder took the watch to see what offer he could get. The potential buyer took the watch, examined it very carefully, and then said, "Sorry, sir, but this is an imitation—it is not the real thing."

<u>History</u>

The church at Sardis, which Jesus instructed John to write about, thought they were actually alive, but in reality they were dead. Sardis is the name of one of the most talked about cities of the ancient East. It had a 2000-year history and was the ancient capital of the kingdom of Lydia. [18] The city also was famous for wealth and wisdom. Thales, the first Greek philosopher, and Solon, the great Greek legislator, were citizens of Sardis.

Croesus was once the king of this great city. He brought the city to greatness and also lived to see his work brought down to disaster. The city had been built on top of a 1500-foot high plateau with steep cliffs on each side. She stood there overlooking the Hermes Valley as a giant impregnable fortress. No apparent approach to the city could be used by an invading army. Beginning at this point, we have a very interesting story.

King Croesus wanted to go to battle against Cyrus, king of Persia. He consulted the famous oracle of Delphi about his intentions and was told, "If you cross the River Halys, you will destroy a great empire. He took this advice to mean that he would destroy the Persians. However, the outcome was that Croesus was the one to be destroyed.

The king crossed the river and was put to flight. He was not too worried, however, and simply withdrew to his impregnable fortress of Sardis to recoup.

Cyrus laid siege to the city. After 14 days of siege, Cyrus promised a rich reward to any soldier who could find a way to enter the city. [19] He had in his army a Mardian soldier named Hyeroeadis, who had been watching Sardis. He saw a soldier accidentally drop his helmet over the edge of a cliff. He saw this soldier slowly and carefully climb down the cliff to retrieve his helmet and then climb back up to the top.

That night this observing soldier led a party of hand-picked men up this same way, and when they reached the top, they found the city unguarded. The people of Sardis assumed they were so safe that no guard was necessary. The city was easily defeated, and it vanished from history for 200 years under Persian rule.

Alexander the Great was next to rule the city and made

it a place of culture. After he died, Antiochus the Great became the ruler over Sardis. He laid siege to the city of Sardis for a year, and finally they took the city the same way. Again, Sardis was defeated because her people felt too secure to need a guard to watch.

A city with this history would understand what Christ meant when He said, *"Be alert, and strengthen what remains, which is about to die, for I have not found your works complete before My God. Remember, therefore, what you have received and heard, keep it, and repent. But if you are not alert, I will come like a thief, and you have no idea at what hour I will come against you."* (Rev. 3:2)

The church of Sardis was a degenerate church in a degenerate city. The church, like the city, had a name for life, but was dead.

Sardis, like the other churches John writes about, was a representative church. It represented the church period of history when the Thyatiran period of church and state union merged into the dark ages and was finally restored through the Protestant Reformation. The date of this era of Sardis is about 1517-1750 A.D. Theologians who encourage the union of church and state should remember the Dark Ages. In this regard, the history of Sardis is usually woven into the history of the church.

Attribute

When Christ came to address a problem in a church, He revealed an attribute about Himself that would be a solution and encouragement to the church. He addresses the church at Sardis and says, *"The One who has the seven spirits of God and the seven stars."* (Rev. 3:1).

Jesus tells us in Rev. 1:20 that the seven stars are the angels (messengers, pastors), and the seven spirits are from the Holy Spirit of God. These references symbolically speak of the Holy Spirit in the scope of His power and perfect work. Isaiah expressed this in Isaiah 11:2: *"And the Spirit of the Lord shall rest upon Him the spirit of wisdom, and understanding, the spirit of counsel and might, the spirit of knowledge and of the fear of the Lord."* Christ would have the church at Sardis to know that He desires to guide His church by the effectual working of the Holy Spirit. In Rev. 1:4-5 the same spirits are linked with the Eternal Father and with Jesus Christ as the only source of grace and peace. The prophet Zerubbabel would have reminded the church at Sardis: *"Not by might, nor by power, but by my spirit, saith the Lord of Hosts."* (Zech. 4:6 KJV).

He also reminds the church that the leadership "seven stars," the oversight brethren, are in His right hand (Rev. 1:16, 20). Our God is a jealous God. He is jealous for the relationship He wants to have with us to give us His very best. The church thought they were alive, but Christ's observation of their condition said they were dead. Lacking were the strength and power they needed to cope with the everyday lifestyle.

A friend was recently diagnosed with cancer. His first question to the medical team was, "how long?" The staff said, for some, 16 months, others 20 years. He only heard the months and immediately began to make final plans. His life became obsessed with anxiety and frustration. It was obvious that the spirit of grace and peace was not at work in his life. He was dealing with his problem in the human spirit. When we deal with life's problems in the human spirit, we can only do what we can do. When we let God work with us in the power of the Holy Spirit, we get what God can do (Matt. 6:7-8).

Tells Us to Pray Matt. 6: 7-8

Before returning to the Father after His resurrection, Jesus made a promise to his followers in John 16:33: *"I have told you these things so that in me you may have peace. You will have suffering in this world. Be courageous, I have conquered the world. If you love me you will keep my commands. And I will ask the Father and He will give you another Comforter to be with you forever. He is the Spirit of Truth. The world is unable to receive Him or know Him. But you do know Him, because He remains with you and will be in you. I will not leave you as orphans. I am coming to you."*

Sardis had relied on their past reputation and thought they could never be conquered. Their strategic location sitting high with protective cliffs on three sides gave them a false sense of confidence. In the sports world, we often hear a winning coach tell his team to just concentrate on today's game, forget the victory of last week, and quit thinking about the next team you are going to play. Focus on the present. A great percentage of our worries is over our "What ifs?" We worry a lot about the future. Jesus taught us to pray, "*Give us this day our daily bread.*" (Matt. 6:8).

Commendation and Condemnation

False Assessment

The church at Sardis thought they were doing great. The church had a fine reputation, but was presently dead and was living on this past reputation. I am sure they were surprised to hear this word of criticism. Didn't they have the finest pastor, ceremonies, deacons, teachers, singers, and leaders to be found anywhere? Yet with all their talent and activity, they were called "dead."

Sardis was filled with people who, for all practical and spiritual purposes, were dead (a form of godliness, denying the power, 2 Tim. 3:5). Paul said, "*Men are dead in trespasses and sin.*" (Col. 2:13). The Sardis church was a dead and indifferent orthodoxy. No Jezebels, Balaamites, or Nicolaitans were present. Everyone was too dead to cause controversy. The people were so ineffective that they had ceased to matter in the life of the community. Unbelievers saw no difference in them. Christians engaged in the same activities as the outside world. They did not want to give anything up since they saw that doing so made no difference in the average Christian. We live in a "dry-eyed" society. No one weeps over sin, sinners, lostness, or godlessness. Are we dead? The church had settled down during the time of Constantine without persecution or challenge, and because of national acceptance, they lost their witness and power.

The Escaping Ones

The word Sardis means "the escaping ones" or "those who came out." [20] Now Jesus recognizes a remnant. *"Thou hast a few names even in Sardis that have not defiled their garments."* (Rev. 3:4). Once again, Christ is saying that you don't have to fit into the characteristics of the age. You can be different from all the others. These days were dark, but you can be a light that shines through the darkness. These are days of defilement, but you don't have to defile your garments. Even in the darkest times God has His leaders.

The Reformation

The intolerable rule and authority of a corrupted papal regime reached its climax on October 31, 1517. Martin Luther nailed his 95 theses to the church door in Wittenberg, Germany. The Protestant Reformation was born. Zwingli, in Zurich, Switzerland, and John Knox of Scotland took up the cause and light began to shine once again through the darkness. These men were followed by Peter Waldo, John Wycliffe, Balthasar Hubmeir, Girolamo Savonarola, John Bunyan, and many others who had not defiled their garments.

Application

Christ gave instruction to these few at Sardis: *"Be watchful and strengthen the things which remain."* (Rev. 3: 2). He calls for them to "wake up." There were at least 3 different groups in the church: those who who had never experienced Christ—the lost, carnal Christians, and those who loved God. Paul reminded the Ephesians to *"Get up, sleeper, and rise up from the dead and the Messiah will shine on you."* (Eph. 5:4). Keep on remembering, and don't forget it, for this is strengthening! Repent and hold it fast.

Promises

Clothed in Righteousness

Be an overcomer. You will be clothed in white garments. The ministry is referred to as a "profession of the cloth." For that reason, when a minister was excommunicated, he was referred to as "defrocked." When John Huss was burned at the stake, his garb was torn off and burned first. Christ says they may burn your garb, defrock you, or try to defile your garments, but you will walk with me clad in white robes of righteousness, which I will provide.

Permanent Residents

He also promises to not blot out our names from the Book of Life. Those were days of excommunication. People were consigned to Hell. Therefore, they lived in great fear. When the papal legate stood before Savonarola, he lifted his hand and said, "I separate thee from the church militant and from the church triumphant." Savonarola replied, "From the church militant, yes, but from the church triumphant, never, for it is not in thy power to do so."

Reward

Martin Luther was excommunicated by the Roman Catholic Church and consigned to Hell and damnation. But God said, "I will not blot out your name." The practice in cities like Sardis was that when you were born, your name was written in a book of life.[21] If you lived as a worthy citizen, nothing happened to change that. However, if you committed some terrible wrong and brought shame on yourself and the city, your name was blotted out as if you had never lived. Christ promised that He would never treat one of His children like that. He not only holds the church leadership in His right hand, but through them He holds each member in the eternal grip of His hands.

Wake Up and Come Alive

He further promises that if you confess Him and are true to Him, He will confess you. The Lord will read the list of names from the Book of Life to His Father and say, "These are mine."

To this church where Jesus had very little to say good about them, He admonishes the "few" who have not been defiled to be alert, to wake up. The reason a church dies is that they change their focus from closely following on a daily basis the Lord Jesus, and they become focused on "doing" rather than on "being."

He tells them to "strengthen the things that remain." He wants them to "build up." God always has maintained a remnant. He does not need the multitude to accomplish His work. Jesus spent three years working closely with only twelve. If you are in a situation that is small in number, then concentrate on building them up, whether two or twenty-two.

How to Come Alive

When death occurs, there is a separation of the spirit from the body. In the church—the body of Christ—when death occurs there is the separation of the spirit and there is no power, no dynamic, and no strength. When a person invites Christ into their life, the Holy Spirit comes to live within the person alongside the human spirit. When the human spirit is not submissive to the leadership of the Holy Spirit, the strength is gone. So Christ tells the faithful few at Sardis to "power up."

<u>Application</u>

Clean Up

Again He instructs them to *"keep what you have received."* (Rev. 3:3). He wants the church to hold fast to the doctrines. Do not waver from the strong truths, for these are the anchors of the soul that can weather the storms of life. There are only two commandments to remember. *"Love the Lord thy God with all thy soul, mind and strength, and [love] thy neighbor as thyself."* (Luke 10:27).

Christ reminds them to *repent*. He wants them to clean up their lives so that others can clearly see Him in them, and if they follow these encouraging words, He makes two promises to them. First, He will not blot out their name in the Book of Life, and secondly, He will confess them to the Father. Again, He simply will say to the Father, "These are mine."

Wake Up

Churches die when they worship the past rather than addressing the present and future. They also die when they become overconfident in their strength and forget that spiritual power and strength comes from the Lord. They are in danger of dying when they let down their guard and allow the enemy to come in unchallenged.

Listen Up

Churches tend to take on the culture of the area where they exist. If they are to change that culture to be what God wants it to be they must listen and "hear" what the Spirit is saying through the preaching and teaching of the Word of God. Also, they must serve as a role model of the Christian life before those outside and be compassionate confronters as a change agent for those inside. Do you remember the story of the watch, the Patek-Phiilppe? The world is waiting to see if you are the "real thing."

The world is watching the Christians, and they want to see how they respond when adversity strikes. If the Christian buckles under and acts like an unbeliever complaining with a "Why did this happen to me?" attitude, then the unbeliever will say, "It is not real—I see no difference." But if believers hold their heads and hearts up high, the unbelievers will be convinced that Christianity is real.

Love Up

In adversity, it is important that fellow Christians remember the needs of others. When adversity comes, and it will, believers need the love of other believers; they need to be encouraged to lay hold of their faith in a God who loves them, and they need hope: *"That to live is Christ but to die is gain."* (Phil. 1:21). Love, Faith, Hope—these are the weapons of our warfare as children of God.

Jesus, on His return to be with the Father, promised to

send the Holy Spirit. He has fulfilled that promise. When the Spirit came, He gave spiritual gifts to the believers. These gifts were the equipment the church needed then, and still needs today to meet the challenges our culture faces. Discover your spiritual gift, and start using it as a valuable weapon for change in the culture around you.

STUDY GUIDE

F- Found. Jesus said to this church, *"I have not found your works perfect before God."* What did He mean by this? What works?

A- Alive. *"You have a name that you are alive, but you are dead."* How can a church be both dead and alive?

I- *"I will confess his name before My Father."* Who is Jesus talking about? What must you do to have Him confess your name before His Father?

T- Truth. What truths do you find in this letter that are helpful to you in your walk with Jesus?

H- His name. What does it mean to have one's name blotted out of the Book of Life? Can this ever happen to a true believer in Jesus? Why or why not?

Chapter 6

DIFFERENCE MAKER

~

The Church at Philadelphia
(Revelation 3:7-13)

Introduction

Whe autumn comes in many states it marks the beginning of a popular sport—deer hunting. Preparation for this begins many months before as hunters purchase equipment, practice their aim, and begin researching the hunting area.

The season in many states opens with bow hunting. This requires climbing a stand, usually a tree, while wearing camouflage to blend in with the landscape and patience. The hunter waits and waits, and then the moment comes.

A ten-point buck is moving into the area. The hunter

has his bow on ready, but he waits for just the right moment. He knows he will only have one chance to bag this trophy. He patiently waits, and he knows that he must react or lose the opportunity. The door to this opportunity may only be open this one moment in time. We have but one life to make a difference for eternity. Doors that open to us must be used wisely and in timely fashion. Jesus saw this in the church at Philadelphia.

Historical Background

A City of an Open Door

Philadelphia was the youngest of the seven cities and was founded by colonists from Pergamum under the reign of Attalus the Second. *Philadelphos* is the Greek word for "one who loves his brother." Attalus had such great love for his brother, Eumenes, that they called him *Philadelphos*. From him, Philadelphia received its name.[22]

The city was founded for the specific purpose of spreading Greek culture and language to Lydia and Phrygia. It was so successful that by 19 A.D. Lydia had forsaken their own language and had become Greeks. The city was considered an open door for the spreading of Greek culture. So when Jesus said to the church, *"I have set before you an open door,"* they would know that they were being given a new missionary opportunity to spread the Gospel of Christ (Rev. 3:8). This church, like all the other six, was chosen because it was representative of a certain period of church history, the 18th-20th centuries, or 1750 A.D. until now.

A City of Earthquakes

A great earthquake destroyed this city along with Sardis and ten other cities in 17 A.D. [23] In these other places, the quake struck and was over with, but in Philadelphia the tremors continued for years. For that reason, it was truly a city of earthquakes. Shock waves were felt daily. The people feared lest at any moment they, along with what remained, would be swallowed up. Some citizens moved to the edge of the city to escape falling stones. Others in the city actually lost their minds. Still others, living in the city, would flee to the countryside every time a tremor was felt. The people were ever going out in flight and then returning to the city—a constant going out and coming in.

A City with Many Names

When the earthquake first struck, Philadelphia was destroyed. Tiberius, the Roman Emperor, furnished the funds to have it rebuilt. The people were so grateful that they named the city *Neocaeserea*, meaning "the new city of Caesar." The name was later changed again to "Flavia" in honor of Flavius Vespasian. So, when Jesus said, *"I will write upon him my new name,"* the believers would understand (Rev. 3:12).

It Was a Great City

When every other city had fallen, Philadelphia still stood. For centuries it was a free Christian missionary city in the midst of a pagan people. It was the last stronghold of Asian Christianity. Today, there is still a Christian testimony there.

The Attribute of Christ for Philadelphia

Jesus is the Holy One, the True One, the One who has the key of David, who opens what no one will close, and closes what no one can open (Rev. 3:7). This description is of God Himself. Throughout the Old Testament, God is the Holy One. *"Holy, Holy, Holy, is the Lord God of Hosts."* (Isa. 6:3). This title of holiness confirms the fact that the Son and the Father are one, and *"the one that has seen me has seen the Father."* (John 14:9). He is the True One. We find in Him no shadow of turning. Jesus is the same yesterday, today, and forever (Heb. 12:8). He is the way, the truth, and the life (John 14:6).

He also has the Key of David. This is a reference to Eliakim, the steward to Hezekiah. He was given a key to the palace and the treasure (Isa. 22:20-25). No one could approach the king except through Eliakim. Nor could they take anything out of the treasure store except through him. So here, Christ is revealed to have the key to everything. He has the key to Hell, the grave, our lives, and to heaven. He alone can open, He alone can close, and no one else can close or open. He has the key to all the treasures that are stored up for every believer. With this thought, He makes a transition in verse 8 and says to the church, *"I have set before you an open door."*

Commendation or Condemnation

Jesus notes that they *"have a little strength, they have kept His word and not denied His name,"* hence the open door of missionary opportunity (Rev. 3:8). The church history of this era (1750 A.D. to present) gives adequate testimony to those who have walked through this open door.

Some descriptions of this church era are: missionary expansion, evangelism, Bible societies, and worldwide preaching of the Gospel from 1750 until now. William Carey became the father of the modern day missionary movement by being the first missionary to India in 1792. His life's story reads like a great spiritual, providential romance. Another missionary, Adoniram Judson, in 1813 went into Burma with the gospel of Christ. His friend, Luther Rice, traversed our land raising money and pleading for the people to become missionary-minded. All of these and many others, like Lottie Moon in China, gave their very lives to spreading the good news to other countries.

Promise and Application

"Because you have kept my Word I will keep you from the hour of temptation which shall come upon all the earth."

(Rev. 3: 10). This is a reference to the tribulation and the great tribulation that shall come upon the entire world. He promises to take His own out of this world before that great and terrible day. Note the word *hour.* The church will not be here for any of it.

Jesus said, *"I will make you a pillar in the temple of my God."* [24] (Rev. 3:12). John saw no temple in heaven, for the Lord God and the Lamb *are* the temple therein. What is a pillar? It is strength, beauty, adornment, and communication. An example is that the believers—the church—are called the pillars of the truth. Another example is that Peter, James, and John are called pillars of the church (Gal. 2:9). Now we—today's believers—are pillars of the temple of God, chosen to adorn and communicate the grace and mercy of Jesus Christ for eternity.

"You should go no more out." (vs. 12). This is a reference to the fleeing during the earthquakes. This meant stability and serenity to the residence of the city and church. There will be no more fleeing, no more anxiety, but just stability and security.

They had now been given the name of their Master. Masters would brand their slaves with their own name. They had their own brands for their sheep. God has placed His badge on us. Also, the name of the city of Jerusalem had been changed often. Its citizens were now given citizenship in the New Jerusalem. He continues by saying that He will also give to us a new name. *"God has highly exalted [us] and given [us] a name that is above every name, that at the name of Jesus every knee should bow and proclaim Jesus Christ as Lord."* (Philippians 2:11). (Note: This interpretation is possible in the light of Romans 8:16: *"Now if we are children, then we are heirs—heirs of God and co-heirs of Christ."* (NIV).) These co-heirs, or joint heirs with Christ, are the Overcomers.

God has uniquely created every person. No two are alike. He also has created each person for a distinct purpose. So every individual is a person of great value. The open door for the church is not only to share the gospel to every person but also to assist every person to become what God designed them to be.

Mankind is created a tripartite being (I Thess. 5:23) with a body—a house to live in, a soul made up of the mind to think with and a will to make choices and emotions to feel with, and an eternal spirit. When an individual comes to embrace Christ as Savior, the Holy Spirit comes to live inside that person alongside their human spirit. The Spirit is there to guide in each of the three areas of the soul.

He also gives to each individual a spiritual gift or gifts to be used in service for the kingdom. Every believer is qualified and equipped to be a "difference-maker." God will use all our difference-making for Him to make a difference in us and others while conforming us to the image of Christ.

The transformation in our life is to be utilized in the

sharing with others who are unbelievers. Christ's last message to the church was: "*All authority has been given to me in heaven and on earth. Go, therefore and make disciples of all nations, baptizing them in the name of the Father, and of the Son and of the Holy Spirit, teaching them to observe everything I have commanded you, and remember I am with you always to the end of the age.*" (Matthew 28:18-20).

This means we are to use every resource possible to get the gospel message to the nations. It also means that some are called *to go* with the message.

There are those who cannot go but can provide the means for others to go. All can use the weapon of prayer that doors open now will be walked through by those who have been willing and led to go. Believers need to evaluate their resources and seek God's leadership as to where they can be invested to yield the greatest results. There are many organizations with their hands out for these resources. Believers need to be wise and remember the command from Christ was to support the local church. Our tithe belongs to the local church where we are receiving spiritual nurture. Our missionary giving to assist others who are going needs to be through the local church as well. Remember that the only thing you can take to Heaven with you is the person that has become a believer because you invested your life and resources to tell them about the saving power of Jesus Christ.

STUDY GUIDE

F- Fast. Jesus told this church to *"hold fast to what you have."* To what does this refer? Are these virtues that you are holding fast?

A- An open door. What is this open door? Does Jesus have open doors for us today? Give examples.

I- *"I will . . ."* Make a list of all the "I will" statements Jesus makes in this letter. Notice how He makes these promises that apply to us today.

T- Trial. Notice the term "hour of trial." How do you interpret this? Can Christians today expect times of trial because of their faith? Give examples.

H- The New Jerusalem. What is this "New Jerusalem"? Find other references to this in Revelation.

Chapter 7

RELIGIOUS AND REPULSIVE

~

The Church at Laodicea
(Revelation 3:16-22)

Introduction

Here is an old home remedy for sore throat.: Place two tablespoons of salt in a glass of heated water. Gargle it in your throat. Caution! If the solution is tepid, it will do no good and may even cause nausea.

The only occasion where we read that Christ could become sick was when He saw the lukewarm church at Laodicea.

History

Laodicea was founded by Antiochus II in 261-246 B.C. [25] It was a city of wealthy bankers and financiers. The many millionaires combined to build theatres, huge stadiums, lavish public baths, and fancy shopping centers. The city lay on one of the great Asian trade routes, and this insured its great commercial prosperity. They were wealthy enough that when an earthquake destroyed much of the city in 60 A. D., they refused Rome's financial help. *"I'm rich; I have become wealthy and need nothing."* (Rev. 3:17).

Great Medical Center

Laodicea was also the home for a great medical school. The temple was used as the medical school. So famous were the doctors that the names of some were on the coins of Laodicea. It was famous for the manufacturing of a pill called Tephra Phygria, which was sold all over Asia Minor and the Roman Empire. The patient would crush it into powder and make an eye salve to be used for some common eye diseases. Eye salve was available for the physical, but many in Laodicea were spiritually blind.

Nearby was the city of Hierapolis, famous for its hot springs and mineral water. The city of Laodicea received their water from Hierapolis. Pipes were also laid to bring the hot springs' mineral water into Laodicea. At certain times the water arrived hot, and at other times it was tepid. It was never very dependable. Citizens just tolerated the lukewarm mineral water.

Area of Mineral Springs

In the district of Laodicea and Hierapolis were many warm mineral springs. A weary traveler, hot and thirsty, would come to one of these wells thinking to quench his thirst. He would take a big drink of this refreshing looking water. The surprised drinker discovered it to be so lukewarm that he became nauseated, and in disgust and disappointment he spewed the mineral-laden water out of his mouth.

Christ uses this example as a point of criticism to the church. He says as a church they were neither cold nor hot. Therefore, they were a nauseating disappointment. He said, "*I would that you were either cold or hot.*" (Rev. 3:15).

Be Palatable

A lot of speculation exists as to why God would rather have a cold church than a lukewarm one, all of which is beside the point. He isn't saying to be hot spiritually or cold spiritually, but rather be palatable. Don't be a disappointment! Be appetizing. Be refreshing. Be what you were meant to be. They were being condemned by Christ for their indifference.

Indifferent to Doctrine

They were indifferent to doctrine. Their indifference expressed itself in doctrinal broad-mindedness, liberal theology, social gospel for civic betterment, a form of godliness and no power, ever learning but never coming to the knowledge of truth, and the abandonment of fundamental orthodoxy. These were a people, both student and teachers, having itching ears, bragging egos, and were sentimental do-gooders—all of which makes God sick.

Identified with the World

These people were identified with the world. One outstanding preacher said, "I am overwhelmed with the identity of the Christian with the world. I cannot, for the most part, see any difference in them." The church at Laodicea had lost their identity. Indifference is a malady that brings death to business, governments, powers, communities, church, and Christians. Real dynamic religion calls for fire in our bones. Jesus said, *"If you are not for me, you are against me, and he that gathered not with me scatters abroad."* (Luke 11:23).

A City of Great Wealth

Laodicea was a banking and financial center. The city was so wealthy and self-sufficient that it refused help from the Roman government during the great earthquake of 60 A.D. The people rebuilt her without help. They were saying, *"We have need of nothing, for we are rich and have increased with goods."* (Rev. 3:17). The city was convinced of her wealth, but blind to her spiritual poverty. The church had taken on the culture of the city.

A City of Clothing Manufacture

They raised sheep that were famous for their soft, black, and glossy wool. This city made the finest garments in the world. These garments and wool were sold all over the Roman world. They adorned themselves lavishly on the outside, while they had nothing to hide their inner ugliness and nakedness of soul.

Attribute

The Amen

Christ introduces himself as *"The Amen, the faithful and true witness, the originator of God's creation."* (Rev. 3:14).

The word *Amen* is translated in both Greek and English, meaning truth.[26] *"Know that Yahweh your God is God, the faithful (amen) God."* (Deut. 7:7). *"Whoever is in the Land will be blessed by the God of truth."* (Isa. 65:16). This is one of Christ's official titles. He is God's last word; there is no improving on Him. *Amen* is reflected upon the very image of Christ. *"For in Him dwells all the fullness of the Godhead bodily."* (Col. 2:9). He is the Amen.

Morgan states it simply: "It must ever be remembered that He did not say, 'I teach the truth,' nor, 'I declare the truth,' 'I explain the truth,' but 'I am the truth.'" The Amen is the conclusion, it is the finality of nourishment, the perfection of edification, the last word, the end, and to which nothing can be added .[27]

The Faithful and True Witness

A witness must meet three conditions. He must be reliable and honest. He must have seen what he relates. And he must be able to relate what he sees. Christ can tell of God, because He is from God. He is both the Son of God and God the Son. Since God is all knowing and is the "Amen," whatever He speaks about the church or any subject is correct. What He says will be exactly true, because He is in Himself absolute truth, and there is nothing beyond Him in all the realm of truth.

The Originator of God's Creation

This description doesn't mean that He was created. Rather, the meaning is that He is the agent of the creation of God. This fact is firmly established by Scripture. *"All things were made by him, and without him was not anything made that was made."* (John 1:3; Col 1:13, 18). So to the church at Laodicea Christ addresses Himself as one incapable of failure.

Leaving the description of Christ, we come next to consider the city and the church. Once again, we can see how the character of the city is woven into the fabric of the church.

<u>Commendation or Condemnation</u>

The people in the church of Laodicea said:

We are rich - God said, you are poor.

We are increased with goods - God said, you are wretched.

We have need of nothing - God said, you are miserable.

We have eye salve - God said, you are blind.

We are well dressed in our woolen garments - God said, you are naked.

Jesus came into our world not just to condemn us. We bring our own condemnation upon ourselves when we live like the people of Laodicea. Yet even then our Savior stands ready to give compassion, love, and counsel to advise us. He says to Laodicea, *"Buy from me gold refined in the fire, so that you may be rich."* (Rev. 3:18). The idea is this: *and then you will really be rich.* If wealth is the only thing a person has with which to meet the issues of life, he is poor. However, if he has faith that has been tried and tested, he is rich.

He further counsels them to buy white clothes so that their nakedness will be covered. For sure, He is referring to the righteousness that is given to us when we are converted and become believers. It is His righteousness that covers the tragedies in our life as a result of our sin. He adorns us with His imputed righteousness.

He continues to express His care for us when He advises the Laodiceans to get the eye salve from Him so they can truly see. Wisdom is seeing everything from God's point of view. *"Wisdom is supreme, so get wisdom, and whatever else you get, get understanding."* (Prov. 4:7). We get that when He opens our blinded eyes to spiritual truth. Satan and the world put blinders on us. The unbeliever and believer cannot see the traps that the enemy has laid before them. Christ opens our eyes to the truth and then gives us the power and strength to be overcomers. Jesus reminds them that His rebukes and discipline are acts of His love for them. Then He issues an invitation. *"Listen, I stand at the door and knock. If anyone hears my voice I will come in and have dinner with him, and he with me."* (Rev. 3:20).

Three times in the earthly ministry of Jesus He came to a home as a guest and left as the host. The first occurrence was at the wedding in Cana where they ran out of wine. Jesus and His disciples were attending this wedding when Mary, his mother, told Him that they had run out of wine. It is not known why this occurred, but it was an embarrassing situation for the family that was hosting the wedding. It was not the responsibility of the guest to provide wine for the wedding. However, on this occasion, Jesus, as a guest, became the host and furnished the wine (John 2).

The second occasion happened after His resurrection on the Emmaus road with two very disappointed and confused followers (Luke 24:13). They had hoped that Jesus would have been the Messiah. They had witnessed the crucifixion and thought all their hope was lost. Jesus opened their blinded eyes with the Word of God, speaking to them from the Law, the Prophets, and the Psalms. When they reached their home they invited Him to be their guest and He accepted. As they came to the meal, He was the one who broke the bread and blessed it. This was a task that a host would do. So here, Jesus entered the home as a guest but then became the host.

The third experience is before the church at Laodicea. He stands at their door and knocks, and if anyone hears His voice and will open the door, *"I will come in and eat with him, as a Guest, and he with me,"* as the Host. The bottom line for all of this is that when you invite Christ into any problem, difficulty, or disaster in your life, He will come in and take over.

Breakfast was a crust of bread in wine. Noon meal was a hasty lunch at work. Supper was the main meal of the day. Here they would linger long at the table for talk, fellowship, and rest. This is the practice that Jesus desired in this invitation. He also desires that today. Note the individual responsibility: "if any man." The appeal to overcomers in all seven of the churches is addressed to the individual. The message is to the churches in general. The commendation is to the group. The condemnation is to the whole body, but the appeal to overcomers is in the singular. Each person is an individual. He must act for himself. He must eat for himself, sleep for himself, trust Christ for himself, die for himself, and be judged for himself. So regardless of how everyone else might be overcome by the circumstances and trends, you can be an overcomer.

A Challenge and Conclusion

To **Ephesus** He said, *"You have left your first love, but to him that overcometh I will give to eat of the tree which is in the midst of the paradise of God."* (Revelation 2:7).

To **Smyrna** He said, *"I know the blasphemy of them who say they are Jesus and are not. To him that overcomes will not be hurt of the Second Death."* (Revelation 2:11).

To **Pergamum**, He said, *"Thou hast them that hold to doctrine of Balaam and the Nicolaitans. To him that overcometh I will give to eat of the hidden manna, a white stone and a new name."* (Revelation 2:17).

To **Thyatira**, He said, *"Thou allowest Jezebel to teach and seduce, but he that overcomes will I allow to rule over the nations with a rod of iron."* (Revelation 2:26-27).

To **Sardis**, He said, *"A name to live, but dead. He that overcomes will be clothed in white raiment and I will confess him to my father."* (Revelation 2:5).

To **Philadelphia**, He said, *"He that overcometh I will make a pillar in the temple of my God."* (Revelation 2:12).

To **Laodicea**, He said, *"Overcomers here are granted to sit with Jesus in his throne and to reign with him forever and ever."* (Revelation 2:21).

We have now come to the church that describes the tragic end of the church age. The Laodicean church could best be described as a half-hearted, lukewarm, compromising congregation. So what did the members of this church need to do on a practical basis to change their culture? What do you need to do to change the culture where you are located?

First, examine your priorities. What is important in your life? How do you spend your time? What or on whom do you center your attention? How do you deal with adversity and conflict? Do you hold grudges? Have you encountered something in your past that has embittered you? Do you practice forgiveness? How much time do you spend in the Word of God? Have you shared your faith with anyone in recent days? Do you maintain an active prayer ministry? What stand have you taken against the evil that exists around you? Do you look at others and make judgments on what you see on the outside? Do you see others as persons of great value and self-worth? Is your approach to life done in humility or in pride and arrogance? Have you submitted yourself to someone as spiritual authority over your life? Are you working toward letting the Word of God and the Holy Spirit teach you the fruits of the Spirit? Are you careful on how you handle your finances? God is watching how you earn money, how you spend money, and how and to whom you give money.

Responding to these questions may lead you to a time of confession and repentance. This can be the beginning of impacting the culture in your personal walk with the Lord and provide the stimulus for becoming an overcomer that Christ has promised to bless. It can be the spark that ignites the flame within the church and results in it becoming the bride adorned with His righteousness and awaiting the Groom's coming. He is coming and will be knocking on the door of your heart. Please open the door.

Christ makes promises to believers in each of the seven churches. He calls them *overcomers*. Persons who have embraced faith in Jesus as their Savior and Lord are overcomers. There is only one perfect overcomer and that is Jesus. He says, *"I also overcame, and am set down with My Father in His Throne."* (Rev. 3:21). We become overcomers when we identify with Him. He said, *"In the world you will have tribulation, but be of good cheer, I have overcome the world."* (John 16:33). John also wrote, *"For whatsoever is born of God overcomes the world; and this is the victory that overcomes the world, even our faith."* (I John 5:4). You can be the change agent God uses to change the darkened culture in your world. Today is the very best day to begin. The thief does not announce his coming; neither does Jesus. But when Jesus does, it will be too late to begin. *"He that hath an ear to hear let him hear what the Spirit is saying to the church."* (Revelation 3:22).

STUDY GUIDE

F- Faithful. Jesus described Himself as one who is "the Faithful and True Witness." What does this mean to you? Does He expect us to be like this?

A- Amen. What does this term mean as applied to Jesus?

I- I. Jesus said, *"I stand at the door and knock."* What door is this and how does He knock today?

T- To. *"To him who overcomes."* What is the meaning of this phrase? Are you an overcomer?

H- Hear. Do you really hear these messages to His church? List some differences these seven letters make for you:

Endnotes

1. (13)
2. (13, p. 234)
3. (13, p.254)
4. (12, p.93)
5. (15 p.298)
6. (7, p. 843)
7. (13, p. 45)
8. (Patterson, NAC p92)
9. (7, p. 842)
10. 11 p.45
11. (*Thlibo* 15, p38)
12. (15 p. 38,155)
13. (13 p. 636)
14. (19 p. 100)
15. (NIV Rev. p111)
16. (10. p110)
17. (12. P50)
18. (7. P.847)
19. (10. p. 120)
20. (9. p. 69)
21. (2. Vol. 1, p. 256)
22. (6 p111)
23. (Vol 2, p. 578)
24. 11, p. 112
25. (7. p.849)
26. (15. p.53)
27. (8, p190)

CPSIA information can be obtained at www.ICGtesting.com
Printed in the USA
LVOW10s2211140416

483706LV00032B/662/P